ZORA'S–
SOMEDAY OVER
THE RAINBOW

IRYNA COLVIN-SPENCER

PERSONAL DEDICATION

This book is dedicated to my family who have been very supportive over the years. My husband Lee, my daughter Julianne and her husband Bill, my son Thaddeus Jr., and my grandchildren on the Piusienski, Renczkowski, and Colvin sides. My sister Mary, my brother Robert (Mike), and all my Chutko, Teluk, Spencer, and Colvin family members. My close, long-time friends, and of course my LIB ladies. Your encouragement has been my light. Thank you all.

ZORA'S DEDICATION

This book is dedicated to Roczen, a young lad of three with a beautiful smile that captured my heart right from the start and will now be forever part of our lives.

I'm also dedicating this book to my entire family and friends. How fortunate I am to have all of them in my life. They all hold a special place in my heart. They say I have unconditional love, but they serve as a constant reminder of what unconditional love is all about.

I would also like to give a HIGH FIVE shout-out to my friend Roczen, his mommy Danielle, and AJ.

Wuff you! High Five! Zora

If you want to judge a person's character, please observe how they interact with your children and fur babies.

Please Donate to Animal Shelters everywhere.

Contents

ACKNOWLEDGMENTS

*To all of these special businesses below who
offered great accommodations and hospitality.*

La Quinta Hotels in: Wytheville, Virginia; Columbia, North Carolina, and Lake Mary, Florida

Hampton Inn Hotels in: Columbia, North Carolina and Weston, West Virginia

*To family and friends who offered their
hospitality and some memorable moments.:*

Anna and Steve, Helen and Jay of DeBary, Florida

Brother, Robert Michael (Mike), and Larry

My sister Mary and brother-in-law Paul

Marge, Mike and (Lulu)

Tom and Judy (Rudy)

Roger and Randy (Echo)

Lori, Kathryn and Sally Ann

Eva and Dance (Seve), Mary (Maria) and Joe

Ihor

A heartfelt special thank you to Jackie from Cy's Pharmacy of Elma, and the Rutkowski family for hosting my first book signing event for "Zora's Letters" in 2018, and then for "Zora's Travels" in 2022.

A special thank you to Becky, of "The Grooming Post", Elma, New York, who has kept Zora groomed to perfection, and to Sherman.

Please support of join your local service organizations: Lions Club; ZONTA; Rotary, or any group that works to help their community.

Thank you all for the memories

PROLOGUE

Zora and Roxy were best friends and fur cousins since they were five months old. Zora was adopted from a woman who aspired to make Zora a show dog. Zora's younger months left her insecure and fearful. She was constantly reminded about what a mistake was made in purchasing her. The woman who had purchased Zora to maximize her returns on her investment, had her dreams shattered, and as a result, she took it out on Zora.

Roxy was purchased from a breeder after her young family actually researched over the internet to find a dog with her qualities and demeanor. When Roxy arrived at her first forever home, she knew she was loved right from the start. Roxy had a family that had a mommy, a daddy, and two girls that fawned over her from the beginning. They lovingly and patiently worked with her to recognize what was acceptable and what was not. She strived to keep her family proud of her accomplishments and learned quickly.

After Zora met her forever family, it took her a couple of days to feel comfortable and loved. Her new parents did everything they could to make her fit right in. She was surprised that upon arriving at her new home, she was no longer caged. The door to her kennel was open, and it didn't take her long to realize she didn't have to stay locked up. When her new mommy took her out, she was allowed to roam on the lawn and explore to her heart's content. Her mommy wasn't letting her use puppy pads in a confined area but daily moved the pads closer to the outdoors, and then it dawned on Zora that's what was expected of her. It took so little to please her mommy that she picked up on what was expected of her within two weeks.

When Roxy and Zora got together, they compared notes and realized that they were both very lucky to live with such loving family members. They now realized they had unconditional love, and it was easy for them to return the same. The two cousins were very fond of each other, and it became natural for them to give each other a hug when they got together, which was quite often. Zora often stayed at Roxy's home when her mother was called out of town. Sissy, mommy's daughter, was responsible for Zora's well-being. Zora loved those visits, as did Roxy. It was during those times that Zora and her mommy started texting. That practice culminated into Zora's first book,

Zora's Letters, a heart-warming book about overcoming uncertainties, unconditional love, and how absence does truly make the heart grow fonder. A few years after COVID restrictions were lifted, the promise her parents made about taking Zora traveling became a reality. *Zora's Travels* was drafted, and along with those travels, a new friendship was forged between Zora and a young two-year-old boy who was recovering from a stroke he had when he was five days old. Zora's "High Five" and Roczen's "High Five" forged their friendship. It was love at first sight for both of them.

CHAPTER ONE

THE HOLIDAYS

Hi Roxy,

We haven't seen each other since Thanksgiving, and I just wanted you to know I miss you. So sorry I didn't come to visit during Christmas, but Mommy said it would be too crowded with people. I don't get it. I'm little, and you're not that big. We don't take up much space. Anyway, the last time we were together we compared notes when we were first adopted by our families. Tell me again how you all met. Since you were a member of this family first, that means you're older than me, so I'll let you go first. Age before beauty.

Wuff you, High Five.

Hi Zora!

You're so silly. I miss you too! Be thankful you weren't here for Christmas. Someone stepped on me, and there were too many people. Also, our family tradition is a meatless Ukrainian celebration so there were no good leftovers like we had at Thanksgiving. I could really go for some turkey and green beans about now. Yum! So, my family found me through a friend. My sister Michala had to write an essay for school about the pet they have or the pet they want. Michala wrote how she wanted a fluffy white dog. My mom said as Michala was reading her essay she had tears in her eyes and wrote such a good essay that they decided to look for a fluffy white dog. They went to the local animal shelters but couldn't find any. Then a friend posted how their dog had a litter of puppies and they were looking for good homes. My mom messaged her friend and the family came to meet me and they said it was fate and love at first site. Did you know that your mom tried to get one of my siblings? None were available though. You got adopted because I was so cute and such a good puppy that your mom decided she wanted a puppy, too. So, you have me to thank for that. Well, I have to go outside now. I'll talk to you later.

Hi Roxy,

You're right about the Christmas dinner, no leftovers for us. For me though, it was all about getting together with family. Your sharing how you were chosen brought back memories of how I came into the family. My mommy told me you were the catalyst for her to once again take a chance on getting a fur baby. She said she decided to look around for someone that really needed a home. Your mom, my sissy, found me online and sent my picture to Mommy. Then my soon-to-be parents and Sissy drove out to check me out. For us it was love at first sight. The lady that was getting rid of me told the family she bought me to be a show dog, but I was a disappointment. As I got older, she realized I wasn't show dog quality. She also said I shouldn't be allowed to have puppies for the same reason. My soon-to-be parents said they wanted me to become part of their family, they weren't looking for a show dog. They paid the lady exactly what she paid for me. The lady gave them the cage she kept me in. At first, on the ride home, I was scared. Sissy was in the back seat, and she took me out of the cage and wrapped me in the blanket because I was shivering so much. Then when I got to my new home the cage was placed in the bedroom, but the door was left open. My new mommy said that I would be allowed to come and go, without being locked up as long as I relieved myself outside. What a change from where I lived before. They only let me out to go on pads and eat. It only took me a week, but I understood what was expected of me. I loved my new home, and never wanted to go back. I was also given a new name, Zora, that I liked right away, it was different. My other name was like jewelry. You were lucky to be in a family that loved you from the start. I was grateful to be saved from someone who didn't, and though I wasn't physically mistreated, there had been no love or attention. My new mommy spent a lot of time holding me, talking to me, and took me for walks. She invited family members to meet me, and most of all we met and became best friends right away. We really are lucky to have our family.

Wuff you. High Five

Hi Zora!

Sorry, it's taken me a while to get back to you. Lately, I've been sore and sleeping more. Being an Eskimo I love the snow. It's so much fun to run in and roll around in, but lately, my legs don't always do what I want them to. My dad had to help me up the stairs yesterday. My mom says that's what happens as we get older. She has a hard time walking, too. She is complaining of back pain. She said it's the weather, but l love the weather. It's better than all the sunshine. I get too hot in the summer. My mom just made some chicken for me, so l gotta go. Bye for now!

Hi Roxy,

Sorry for the delay in getting back to you. It's been a few crazy days here.

First, I had to go to the veterinarians at Seneca Animal Hospital, or as I call it, the one-stop doc. Why is it humans have specialists for every ailment, but we get the same doctor? Are we better off, or are they? Anyway, I digress. My nose was infected, from a UFO. An unidentified flying object. Which means no one was sure how the infection got there. I was given antibiotics, they removed the ugly, dried-up glob off my nose, and sent me home. I must admit it's great breathing without that obstruction. Silly Mommy was putting Vaseline and Neosporin on my nose. Guess she forgot I lick everything off, so none of that helped. The doc did. I feel like a dog again. The antibiotics are working.

In addition to my woes, we had a bit of excitement here. We lost power for a few days, and our electric control box and some main wires had to be replaced. The culprit was human error. Daddy was doing some remodeling, and I guess remodeled a bit more than he expected. Daddy's family and friends kept asking him if he got out of the dog house yet. I didn't even know he had one. After two days, everything was replaced, so things are back to normal again. For now, anyway. How are you doing? Is your mommy feeling better?

Wuff you. High Five.

Hi Zora,

I'm so sorry to hear about your nose. That sounds awful and uncomfortable. Our sniffers are our lifeline. We smell everything from the food we eat to the people we meet.

We're all doing well over here. My mom and I both have been walking a little slow. She says it's from all the rain and arthritis. I can't even jump on the furniture any more and I have a hard time getting in the car going for rides. You're lucky that you're smaller and you can be lifted up. My family lays with me a lot on the floor and still gives me lots of love. I just wish I could run around and jump like I used to. My mom says my dad is in the doghouse sometimes, too. I've never seen it though. My mom said it's a figure of speech when they do something they're not supposed to and cause trouble. Humans are funny. It should be a cat house because cats cause a lot more trouble. Pepper still paws my face when I'm sleeping. I really wish there was a dog house and Mom could send Pepper there. You're lucky you don't have a cat for a sibling. I miss Jingles. He was a good cat, and we played nicely together. Mommy said he crossed the rainbow bridge and someday we'll all be together. I hope your nose is healing and you're feeling better. Write soon. Miss you.

This is Pepper getting ready to pounce. She even looks mischievous.

CHAPTER TWO

A QUEST FOR THE REAL PURPOSE OF LIFE

Hello Roxy,

Sorry, it's taken so long to get back to you. I'm sorry that Pepper treats you like a dog. Get it? Lol. Sometimes these cats think they are so superior. If you ignore her, she may come around.

I've been so busy, with Mommy doing a lot of running around, getting tax information together. I'm glad we don't have to do that; it makes humans act crazy. We had company overnight, my fur cousin that looks like me, but he's a different breed. His name is Coach. Our home is like his second home. He has his own bed here. Anyway, I had to entertain him as my parents had to leave us alone because they had to go buy groceries. Yeah, I'm looking forward to some treats. I'm sending you a picture of Coach and me hanging out. I really must admit I'm quite the hostess. I make sure

I share my food, and water with him, even though he has his own place setting and dishes. He's a pretty cool dog, and we get along just fine nowadays. I'm not as jealous of him as I used to be. He's half our age and was much friskier before. Thankfully, he's a bit calmer and easier to put up with. We finally have a bit more in common, but not like you my favorite cousin. We've been together for almost our whole lives. We know a lot of family secrets, that's what makes us closer. Since Coach was spending time with me, I asked him about what he thought his purpose in life was. He believed it was being cute, cuddling, and obedient. He told me that he had a special collar on him and some kind of hidden fencing that kept him from running away. I asked him why he ran away from home. Didn't he like it there? He then told me, there was a female fur baby across the street that he wanted to visit, and his parents were tired of chasing after him. That's why he has the special collar.

He also asked me if I knew what the fur-babies purpose in life was. I told him that I believed my purpose in life was to be a kind, loving companion to my family, entertain their friends, but most of all, let my family know how special they are to me, and I to them. Kindness and love go a long way to nurturing relationships, and I love my whole family. My parents, their children, grandchildren, and all the fur babies that I know in the family. I've never met Mitsy and Pepper, but I'm sure given the chance, we would get along. We may not be the same breed, or look the same, but we all have similarities. Most of all we love our human parents.

I told Coach I will ask around, and when I find a fur baby that is smarter than us, I will ask if they know what our purpose in life is. I also promised him if I found out, I'd let him know.

Guess what Roxy? I'm so excited because I just found out there's a good chance, I'll be going to Florida next month. I'm looking forward to the trip because we are driving down, and I'll get to see some friends along the way. Mommy said we are all getting older, and may not be driving these long distances much longer. It doesn't seem that long to me. I get to sleep a lot, enjoy the scenery, and smell new scents. I'll let you know if the trip is really a go.

Anyway, I better sign off for now. It's almost dinner time, and I can smell my food being prepared. Let me know what you think of Coach after you see his picture. Who knows, maybe you'll meet one day.

Wuff you. High Five

Hi Zora!

You and Coach look a lot alike. The picture of him when he's listening to you is funny. I love the way his ears go up. I'm glad you two are having fun together. We sometimes watch Max when his dad goes on vacation. He's hyper and always manages to get out of the house and run away. You may recall he was like that at your house when he was visiting. He's cute but has no discipline.

These boy dogs in our family are more hyper, and I think they're annoying. If you go to Florida, I hope you have fun. I don't like long car rides; they make me sick. My belly gets all rumbly, and I don't like it. Things have been calm here, nothing exciting. That's just the way I like it. I do miss my sisters though. They're always out. Either at school, work, or out with friends. Mom says everyone is getting older and doing their own thing. I sleep a lot more now. Going to take another nap. Sweet dreams, I hope.

Hi Roxy,

What do you think of this crazy weather? All this ice, it's like a skating rink. Did you try going outside to relieve yourself in it? You bend a little, and the next thing you know you slid a foot, and your backside is sitting on ice. I've skated more in these last few days than I have in all the years I've been alive. I haven't seen the squirrel family lately. They probably can't run because they'll skid. I'll send you the pictures of the squirrel family. Mommy named them. There's Jack, Jay, Jeff, John, and the female is Jewel. We guess she's the female because she's always bossing the other ones around, and chases them away from the peanuts until she's had her fill. We had a group of people over today from an organization that mommy and daddy belong to. I got all the attention. I loved it. Mommy said I can be the mascot of the group. Whatever that is.

Anyway, I hope it warms up enough so the ice melts. Say hi to everyone.

Wuff you, High Five

Hello Zora!

How lucky you have squirrels to play with. We have a lot of deer in our yard. They eat the bushes and make such a mess. My dad's lucky he has a pooper scooper. I haven't done anything exciting lately. I'm sleepy a lot and my legs give out. I hear you're leaving for Florida soon. How exciting! I'm having chicken soup for dinner tonight. I'm excited!

Hi Roxy,

What a week. Today, I finally had my grooming appointment with Becky. When mommy took me in Sherman came to meet her. Mommy remembers Sherman's name because when she first met him, she said, Sherman Tank. I don't think he looks like a tank. Anyway, he always greets us, and we just love him. You might remember him, he's the friendly one at The Grooming Post. He's also the one I told you came running to Mommy real fast, and he jumped on the counter and slid to the floor. We all laughed after we were sure he was ok. You had to be there to see it. I'll send you his picture, and I'm sure you'll remember him. Mommy was running late, so Becky said she would stay later. This gave me the opportunity to have a real conversation with Sherman since he's exposed to a lot of fur babies. He told me how some come in looking really skinny, and others are really fat. I looked him right in the eye, and asked, "Do you think I'm fat?" He didn't hesitate, and replied, "Nah, just right." The longer we talked, the more I realized he really did pay attention to everyone coming in and out. He then told me about the fur babies that never come back anymore. I asked, "Where do they go?" He then asked me if I knew what our purpose in life was with our human families.

I thought about it while I was being groomed. Afterward, I told him that my purpose in life was to be there for my mommy and family. I am a guard dog and always sound the alarm when strangers come to the door, especially since my new daddy got sick, and Mommy couldn't it answer the door right away. That way whoever was on the other side knew that there was someone at home. Fortunately, I became a part of our family when Mommy needed me most. She found me at a time that was difficult for her.

She had just found out my human daddy was very sick. When she brought me home, she took me out on long walks. She poured her heart out to me and I listened. I stood by and hugged her, and gave her kisses when she cried. She confided in me that she only shed tears in private because she didn't want anyone to know how difficult life can be at times. She talked to me, because I could be trusted not to tell anyone. She didn't want my daddy to see her tears, and she always smiled around him. She told me she and Daddy talked about sharing a sign should one of them become separated from the other. Mommy confided in me that she told him, "how about a shining new penny, that way we will know it's from each other. Daddy told her I'm surprised you didn't ask for dollars. That last long walk before my daddy left us was the most difficult one. There were so many family members at the house, and mommy just said she needed to get out of the house a bit to gather her thoughts. I looked up at her and asked, "why do you need to gather your thoughts, I thought they are always in your head." As if mommy could hear me, she replied, "In a few days it will just be us, but we will always know daddy is near, because he already promised me he would send me a shiny penny any time I need to feel his presence." Afterward, we went back to the house and she acted as if nothing was bothering her. So, I guess my purpose in life is to be there for my mommy, make her smile when she is sad, and always show her how much I love her. I do that by cuddling up to her, and just being my own cute self, Showing off the tricks she taught me.

Sherman looked at me for a while, and then he told me what nobody else did. It's the most beautiful, touching story, but I'll save that to tell you in person. Now, I have to go get my beauty sleep. It's a long ride to Florida, and we have a few stops on the way. Did I tell you I'm going to see Roczen again? He's the little boy who knew my High Five sign and gave it to me when we first met. I touched my paw to his High Five, and we are now friends for life. I hope he remembers me, though I don't see how he could forget. Everyone tells me I'm cute and unforgettable. Anyway, I'm really tired. Good night. Wuff you. High Five.

Hello Zora!

Hope you have fun in Florida. It sounds like you will. I met Sherman before. I get scared going to the groomers. I like Becky but not the dryer, and being away from my family. I was bit once by a big dog in my neighborhood while going for a walk. I was on a leash and he wasn't, and he hurt me badly. There are big dogs at the groomers. Though none of them made any moves towards me, I still have flashbacks to the day I was mauled and almost lost my life. I had to spend a couple of days in the hospital. It was so scary. When you get back home you should come over so we can chase Pepper around the house. That cat thinks everything is all about her. She's even eating my dog food. Hello, it's for dogs, not cats, eat your own food. She's a lot faster than I am. I like it when you're here because she's afraid of you and hides. It's so nice out today. Mommy, Michala, and I sat out on the porch for a while getting some fresh air. Have fun seeing everyone!

CHAPTER THREE

FLORIDA BOUND

Hello Roxy,

It was one of our longest days. Twelve hours of driving, which should have been between eight and nine. The ride started out great. Mommy and Daddy stopped at Cracker Barrell in Meadville, Pennsylvania, for a late breakfast and also to get me a toy because they forgot to pack mine. So much for being organized. My favorite squeaky bone is home alone. So, okay, I forgave them. My new dog toy is a stuffed dog. Ironic, right?

The ride was boring until Pittsburgh, Pennsylvania, where they don't make traveling easy. We were following Route 279, and then it just disappeared. None of their signs indicated it merged with Route 386. Then the GPS system took us back to 279 North instead of 279 South. Then we pulled over to read a map, trying to find Route 79 South. The map indicated that 386 would take us to route 79 South. We first had to get back onto Route 279 South. Are you confused yet? If you heard the volley of conversation between the two adult parents, you would be more confused. Whew! Finally, after an hour or so, we were back on track. Other than a few careless drivers adding stress to our trip, the drive was uneventful. We were all completely exhausted when we pulled into the LaQuinta Hotel in Wytheville, Virginia. We were warmly greeted by a young woman named Brenda, and she made us feel right at home. We took our luggage to our room, then Mommy took me back through the lobby to go outside. On the way back in, we stopped to talk to Brenda, who is so nice. She talked about her fur baby, a terrier named Porky Orky Yorky. She even shared a picture of herself with Porky Orky Yorky. I'm not kidding, that's his name. She told Mommy she had to have surgery, and couldn't have human babies, so now, he's her baby. I could tell she was a really good person, and I sat down by her, and didn't want to leave. Mommy took a picture of Brenda with me and sent her a copy. Despite all the hardships Brenda had in life, she remained strong and sweet.

Brenda wasn't at the desk the next morning, and Mommy couldn't say goodbye to her in person. Mommy did speak to a young lady named Hannah, and asked her to say goodbye to Brenda. I bet if I wasn't already in the car, I would have had a picture taken with Hannah. With my latest grooming, it would have been a great photo. Oh well, next time I'll stick around with Mommy until she takes me to the car. I'm not missing another photo opportunity. We're back on the road again, headed to Columbia, South Carolina. Sending hugs. Wuff you. High Five.

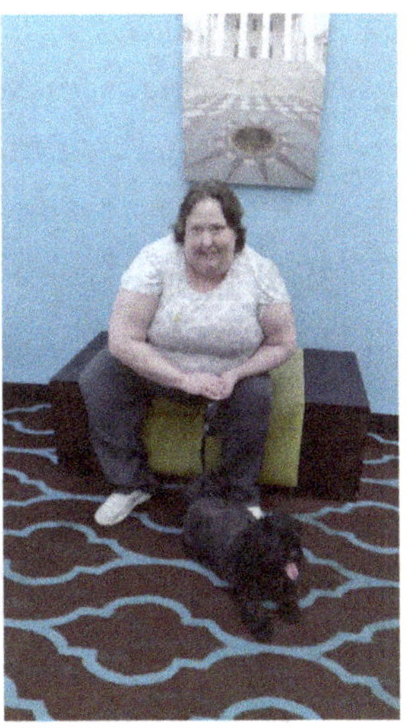

Hi Zora,

Wow! Sounds like you're having fun. Humans aren't as good with directions as we are. I can sniff my way anywhere I need to go. It is so nice here. March and it's still snowing here in good ol' Buffalo. There's enough for me to roll around and play in. Dad even had to shovel. Everyone is saying, "Enough with the snow already. Where's Spring?" I love the snow though. I hope your new dog's squeaky toy looks like Evil Max.

He's always sniffing my butt and jumping on me. I always try to hide from him. He's as annoying as Pepper. I'm glad you and I can have fun and just chill together. I have a stuffed Bengal and chicken I play with. Mommy says I'm good because even though I chew on my toys I don't destroy them. Have fun in the sun and I'll roll around in the snow. I can't wait to hear more about your adventures.

Hi Roxy,

What a frightening ride to Columbia, North Carolina. The fog in Virginia was so thick in the mountains that you could cut it with a knife. It was a paw-biting experience. Then miraculously, after my ears popped, the sun came out. Unfortunately, we couldn't see Rockzen on the way down to Florida. His mother texted Mommy to make revised arrangements on the ride back, as Roczen had a doctor's appointment after his mother got home after working all night. The good news is we will see Roczen and his mother on the way back. The rest of our Columbia highlight was uneventful, with the exception of a touching moment Mommy experienced at Hickory Tavern, which was recommended to Mommy by Adam, at the customer service desk. There was a plaque in the restaurant honoring veterans, which I am sending you. They also had a burger there called the 'Merica Burger, which is served with a small American flag on top. Both my parents had that burger because they said it was for a worthy cause. The restaurant donates $1.00 from each burger purchased to the wounded veteran's organization. What a wonderful, and touching gesture. I think all restaurants should participate in that program. Mommy took a picture of the plaque that was on the wall, which explains why this restaurant honors the veterans, which I am sharing with you. Mommy brought back some of the burger for me, and I scarfed it up. It was yummy.

Next day on the road again, this time to Lake Mary. This LaQuinta Hotel was beautiful and set in a park-like setting. The foyer led right into the main continental breakfast dining area, airy, spotless, and inviting. We had to unpack quickly as we were invited to dinner at Anna and Steve's home in Debary. They are Mommy's adopted cousins from way back. Helen and Jay are good friends of theirs were there also. This group of friends were the ones we saw last year, who together with members of their parish worked tirelessly to help the people in Ukraine. They are still working tirelessly by helping make varenyky (also known as pierogi) and stuffed meat with rice cabbage rolls. Proceeds from the sale of these are sent to aid wounded Ukrainian soldiers.

Also, Myron, Steve's brother was visiting from Southern California. In addition, we were pleasantly surprised that Uncle Mike and Larry drove up from Melbourne. Anna suggested we invite them to their home, and join the festivities. Another great time with everyone, as I was the center of attention, and spoiled yet again. A party to honor my visit, what a perfect way to celebrate my arrival. Whew! I'm now officially full and tired.

Wuff you. High Five

Hello Zora!

Sounds like you're doing a lot. I'm getting tired just hearing about it all. It's always fun getting together with family and friends. My mom's friend, Cheryl, came over Saturday to play cards. She keeps treats in her bag just for me. Her fur baby is a cat, and she doesn't bring any for Pepper, just me. She said if she were to get a dog, she would want one just like me. I feel special. Then TJ came over Sunday with all his paranormal equipment to see if we have spirits in our home. He takes it very seriously and has lots of equipment. Nothing exciting happened with it, which I guess is good, so I just took a nap. It snowed again last night. Everyone keeps complaining about it, but I love it. I'm going to go roll around and play in it before it's gone. Have fun! Wuff you too!

CHAPTER FOUR

AT OUR RELATIVES IN NORTH PORT, FLORIDA

Hi Roxy,

I have to tell you it's very demanding being a celebrity. After taking a photo opportunity with Marian, one of the ladies at the service desk at the La Quinta Hotel in Lake Mary, Mommy thanked the customer service personnel and told them it was one of the nicest hotels on this trip by far. She loved that it was in a secluded spot, close enough to her relatives and Orlando, but far enough away to afford us privacy. We packed up to get back on the road again. We drove, what seemed like forever from DeBary to Aunt Mary's and Uncle Paul's condo in North Port. The projected three-hour drive took a whopping five hours. I was exhausted. It's tough just laying around or glancing out the windows. Sometimes, we saw pelicans, egrets, or herons. These are only a few of the birds we saw. Judging by the birds I am seeing on this trip, I think Florida has more species of birds than we do in western New York. Of course, I don't know that to be a fact, so don't quote me.

It was great pulling up to Aunt Mary's. I felt at home, and I still remembered where I was allowed to go outside when I needed to go. Looks like my memory is still intact. On my walk to my go-to place, we ran into Rudy, and he still remembered me. His parent, Tom, was walking him. We ran up to each other and kissed. I thought he recognized me by sight. He ruined it by sniffing me, but I have no doubt he remembered me. After all, I am unforgettable. You know, unlike humans when they hug someone, they can't remember their name, and call them honey, sweetie, or dearie. How pathetic. Anyway, I'm planning on visiting him before I leave, but this time I'll do the sniffing. Let's see how he likes it.

My parents and relatives decided to take a ride to the Edison and Ford Winter Estates in Fort Myers Florida. Aunt Mary told Mommy dogs were allowed. So, when we got there, we were told only service dogs with papers are allowed. The irony is my service dog papers were in our car, and we drove in Uncle Paul's car. It seems the restrictions were put in place a couple of years ago. I had my picture taken with Aunt Mary by the Edison statue, in front of the Indian Banyan trees. Edison is hiding behind Aunt Mary. What a bummer that was. Daddy wanted to check out the inventions. We then left and took a ride to the Fort Myers Beach area, which had been hit by Hurricane Ian. The hurricane totally decimated the whole beach area. There were yachts in trees, houses off their foundations, hotels destroyed, countless homes and businesses completely destroyed. I've never seen a war zone, but I bet it looks pretty much like what we saw. I'm sending you a couple of pictures so that you can see part of what we saw. It was extremely quiet in the car. Everyone was solemn by what they had just witnessed.

I have so much more to tell you, but I'm exhausted. I am sending you some of the pictures from Fort Myers.

Wuff you. High Five.

Hi Roxy,

I didn't hear from you, so I thought I'd fill you in on what I've been doing. The last few days I went on plenty of walks, and Roger stopped by with Echo to visit. Mommy kept taking pictures of Echo, which gave me a chance to ask him if he knew what our purpose in life was. He told me his purpose was to look handsome, be obedient and loving to his family, and be waited on. He loved being pampered and taken care of. So, his purpose was just to be a good companion. I then relayed to him what Sherman told me about what the dog's lot in life really is. After Roger and Echo left, Mommy looked at all the pictures and burst out laughing hysterically. It seems she took a dozen skewed selfies of herself, and none of Echo. She texted Roger to see if Echo was available before we headed home. I did get a chance to meet with Echo, and he was stunned by the information I provided him. He asked if what Sherman said was true. I told him I had it on good authority that it was. He nodded and smiled.

Hi Zora,

Wow, you really are getting around, and seeing so many things. I guess there are still places where we fur babies aren't allowed, despite the fact that we cause less destruction to property than most humans. We, you and I, were raised with discipline and love. We always were rewarded when we did good, and God, how I hate those words, "bad dog" when we were bad.

However, we learned, didn't we? Of course, after a few minutes of feeling rotten, our human parents hugged us and let us know despite our "accidents, or mischievous side," we were always loved. That said, I'm sorry you were unable to go into the Edison and Ford Winter Estates. It's a good thing your daddy was able to get a picture of you and Aunt Mary near Edison's statue despite the fact that he was mostly hidden behind Aunt Mary. On the bright side, it could have been worse, and the picture could have been really distorted or skewed. See, there's a bright side to everything.

I never really knew that hurricanes could do that much harm. We hear about it on the news, or from others, but you seeing it makes it that much more real. I trust everything you tell me. How sad for all the people and businesses that were impacted by the hurricane. Did you happen to hear if all the fur babies made it to safety, and how they fared in that storm? I pray that everyone was safe, and their lives were spared. It's sad to think they now have to start over, but at least they will have the opportunity to do that.

Nothing really new to report here. It's that pierogi time of the year again, so I'm going to get plenty of rest and ignored for the most part except for food and water and some petting when everyone is too tired to do anything else. Oh well, I guess I should count my blessings, I have a roof over my head, a warm place to lay my head, plenty to eat and drink, and surrounded by family who loves me.

I laughed about the selfies photo incident. That happens here too, sometimes. Not often. I remember your mommy calling Michala or my mommy for help when she has a problem with her phone. This new technology is driving everyone a bit wacky. It's a good thing we don't have to deal with it.

I look forward to hearing about your additional adventures. Love you cuz. Roxy

Dear Roxy,

We've been on a whirlwind tour ever since my last text to you. Let me tell you, while there are many restaurants that allow us on the premises, these establishments have a long way to go to make us feel welcome. I will first tell you all the restaurants I did not go to, but later found out I would have been welcome. My selfish relatives were getting reacquainted with a friend from the Buffalo area and decided I would be too difficult to handle. Me? They actually thought I would be a problem. You and I both know I am extremely well-behaved especially where food is concerned. They met their friend Ihor at the Dockside Waterfront Grill in Venice and then had the audacity to tell me what a great time they had, and how beautiful it was, overlooking the Gulf. To appease me, they brought me some leftovers. Big deal.

The following day we traveled to Largo to meet up with the Picuns and Stavrevski's. The Picun's home was lovely, but no one told me it was to be a feast in my honor. The surprise was great, and I felt like I was special again. The adults sat around and talked about the good old days yet again. Eva's birthday was coming up in a few weeks, and even though she had something to celebrate with the family that was there, the attention was still focused on me. As it should be. After all, I'm the one that made every effort to entertain everybody and made the rounds, where I received a lot of delicious handouts. Mary then told everyone that she and her niece, Eva's daughter, were taking Eva on a cruise to celebrate her eightieth birthday. She said it was girls only. I reminded them I didn't get an invitation. Then I was told we would be back in the Buffalo area when it was time for them to leave on the cruise. So yet again, I was precluded from an adventure of a lifetime, though I'm not sure they allow fur babies on the cruise ship.

It was nice catching up with Mary and Joe and Eva and Dance. I was glad that Seve was not there with them, as I didn't want to keep dodging his attention. I did ask Eva if she would let me have a Zoom call with him, as I had some important information to share with him, that was given to me by Sherman. As usual, Seve, thinking he was royalty, was dressed up in garb to match his personality. In our brief Zoom call, he told me that his purpose in life was to be a great companion to his grandfather, Dance, and entertainment for his grandmother, Eva. That was his lot in life. Despite the fact that I wasn't enamored with him, I liked his answer, as I really liked his grandparents having met them several times. I relayed to him what Sherman told me. Seve actually was quiet on the other end, and I could tell he was letting what I told him sink in. He thanked me and told me that everything makes sense now. We said our goodbyes, and I hung up realizing I had just overcome my negative feelings towards Seve and found I actually liked him.

We had a nice ride back, which took twice as long as going down. Why is it that humans make directional mistakes and then cover that up by saying they intended to take that route so that we could see more of Florida, places we hadn't seen before? The funny thing about all that is that this time Uncle Paul was driving and not Daddy. It must be a man thing about trying to get directions. The irony to all this, everyone had a cell phone, and you would think they would have relied on the GPS system almost immediately upon discovering they weren't heading in the right direction. Finally, either Aunt Mary or Mommy decided to utilize the GPS system, and we got back on track. Actually, I think they both did.

I've been told that tomorrow I am going out to eat out with the family. Will write to you soon, and let you know if that really happens. Hugs to everyone.

Wuff you. High Five.

Hi Zora,

Still pierogi season here, as the orders are being called in. It is still snowing here, along with wicked wind and rain. Even though I do like the cold weather, thanks to my luxurious white fur, I get tired of the dampness and cold weather. Sometimes it's just nice to lay around and let the sun beat on our bodies.

The girls have been busy with school. Daddy is out working a lot of hours. Other than that, my life is bor-

ing compared to yours these days. I do look forward to hearing from you. Have you heard anything about reconnecting with your "High Five" friend Roczen? I know that he is special to you. At least you are having quite the vacation, while I'm still battling snow, wind and rain. Write soon. I'm living vicariously through you.

Hi Roxy,

We did get a chance to eat at Daquiri Deck in downtown Venice. It's a really nice restaurant in the heart of downtown Venice. They are super friendly to us fur babies and let us know we are a welcome addition. Of course, I was recognized for my cuteness and was given an extra treat. This was our last dining out in Venice, before heading home. Tomorrow, I will be getting a chance to visit with Lulu and Rudy, and I will ask them what they believe is their purpose in life, and I will relay to them the wisdom I received from Sherman. I'm making this text short because honestly, I am so tired, and will definitely fall fast asleep before my head hits the pillow.

Wuff you, High Five.

Hi Zora,

We finally received a reprieve from the snow, wind and rain. Actually, it's a nice day to lay around outside. Everyone is home today, and it's nice to have the family together. Mommy's friend Cheryl is coming over to keep Mommy company, and they will be playing some cards. The girls are staying in their room most of the time, with the exception of when Natasha goes to work out, (that means exercise), or when Michala goes to work. Pepper has been a bit more tolerant these days, and though we still don't have the relationship I had with Jingles, I can put up with her aloof attitude. It's better than dealing with her hissing and pawing. Nothing else new to report. I am so looking forward to hearing from you again. It makes me feel like I'm traveling with you. Bye for now Cuz

Hi Roxy,

Sorry it's taken a few days to write you. Yesterday I had a chance to meet with Lulu. I asked Lulu what her purpose in life was, and she said to take care of her mommy and be her mommy's companion and to be a comfort dog. Much like me. She had a similar experience in life, where she lost her human daddy, and then was the sole comfort provider for her mommy until Mike came into the picture. She told me she really likes Mike, and he is very good to her and her mommy. Lulu traveled a lot more than I did, or ever will. She has had the same experiences in the hotels. It was great commiserating with her, and comparing notes. Before I left her, I imparted to her what Sherman told me about our purpose in life. She thanked me profusely, saying it made her feel so much better knowing that. My mommy took a picture of Lulu with her mommy and Mike before we left. We wanted to have it as part of our memories because we weren't sure we'd be returning to Florida and wanted to remember the happy times. Making memories, as mommy likes to call them.

Later that afternoon, Daddy, Mommy and I drove to Bradenton, Florida, to meet Aunt Lori, Kathryn, Sally Ann, and Holly (Sally Ann's fur baby) at Pier 22. It's a beautiful restaurant in Bradenton surrounded by yachts of every size. We had reservations on the deck. It was nice spending some time with the ladies, as they were very good, and long-time friends of Mommy's. Lori and Mommy were friends for over fifty-five years, and Mommy knew Kathryn from a very young age and Sally Ann since birth. Of course, Aunt Lori, as my human siblings refer to her, also has a son, David, whom Mommy has known for just as long. It was a beautiful, sunny day, the water in the Gulf was glistening from the sun, and there was hardly any breeze, the perfect day. Our waiter, Adam, was very entertaining and provided me and Holly with water to cool us down. I asked Holly about her purpose in life. She told me it was to keep her parents company, entertained, and to travel as much as they would allow, which is all the time. I then relayed to her what Sherman had told me, and she lost it. All of a sudden, for no reason that I could think of, she turned on me. She started growling and snarling. Mommy told Sally Ann she couldn't believe that was the same Holly she used to pet and give treats to when she went to visit Lori. Sally Ann was afraid to put Holly down because of the way she was acting. Sally Ann then called her brother Dave, Holly's uncle, and had him pick her up so that we could enjoy the rest of the meal. Of course, I was glad they took Holly after she started growling, I was afraid of her. Sally Ann said that she thought that I looked a little like the dog that had attacked Holly, and that's probably why Holly might have turned on me. My thought was that since she didn't turn on me from the start, it might have been that she didn't like what I told her. She didn't get nasty until I relayed Sherman's wisdom to her. I guess I'll never know. Other than that, we took a few pictures as memories of the day, and I am sharing them with you so that you can be part of my travels. Mommy asked Sally Ann to send her a picture of herself with Holly, as she didn't have the opportunity to take one before the episode happened. I wanted you to see why Holly frightened me. She's bigger than me. We had a wonderful visit, and it was time to leave to go back to Aunt Mary's and Uncle Paul's condo.

The following day, Aunt Mary, Mommy, and I went over to visit with Tom and Judy, Rudy's parents. Actually, Mommy and I went over to say goodbye as we were leaving the next day. I had a chance to have some one-on-one time with Rudy, giving me a chance to ask him about his purpose in his family's life. He told me pretty much what the others said, being a companion, providing entertainment and cuddling, and being an obedient fur baby, that they can appreciate. I then told him what Sherman told me. Rudy came up to me and licked my face and thanked me. He said that this information he will cherish always. You know, it's funny. I received positive feedback from all the fur babies, except from Holly. It made me think that it just may be that she was so distraught about how much I looked like the dog that had attacked her, that she didn't really pay attention to what I had conveyed to her.

We spent a little more time with Tom, Judy, and Rudy, and then Mommy took a picture as a memory keepsake. Saying goodbye to Rudy was tough, as he was my first love.

Tomorrow, we leave for Columbia, South Carolina, where I will meet up with Roczen again. I am so excited. It's going to be hard falling asleep knowing what I have to look forward to, but I'll give it a shot.

Wuff you. High Five

Hi Zora,

All right. You have my full attention. You've told every fur baby so far what Sherman told you, but not to me, your favorite cousin, and best friend. Why is that? On another note, I'm really glad you'll have the chance to get reacquainted with Roczen, and his mommy. I can't wait for you to let me know how that visit went. Also, I'm looking forward to you telling me about my real purpose in life.

Obviously, there's nothing really exciting for me to tell you. Spring is right around the corner, and that means more outdoor fun time. Write soon.

CHAPTER FIVE

RECONNECTING WITH ROCZEN

Hi Roxy,

The ride to Columbia was a bit hairy, and even more paw-biting than I previously wrote to you about. There was a lot of construction, crazy drivers, and worst of all, an accident that held us up for over an hour and a half. There was a backup of traffic on the I75 eastbound, judging from what we saw driving by at least three miles long. Fortunately, for us, we were heading west. Mommy blessed herself when she saw the ambulances, police cars, and fire trucks. She says she always does that, saying a brief prayer for whoever was in the accident, hoping they weren't hurt. Somehow, I don't think that was the case. The cars and tractor trailer appeared mangled. That put a damper on the drive. We made it to the Hampton Hotel almost two hours later than the allotted time we were to meet with Roczen, and his mom, Danielle. Fortunately, Mommy and Danielle kept texting so that she was aware of the new estimated arrival time. The customer service representative, Adam, was very efficient in checking us in so that we didn't have to worry about meeting Danielle and Roczen on time. Danielle made arrangements for us to meet at the Olive Garden near our hotel, to give us time to unpack, and her time to drive up from Lexington, which was about twenty minutes away.

As we pulled up to the Olive Garden restaurant, I spotted Roczen immediately. Danielle, Roczen's mommy, and a young lady, who was introduced to us as Danielle's adopted niece and goddaughter, AJ, met us and we all hugged. We were taken into the restaurant, into a backroom corner where we had the area all to ourselves. Roczen and I played almost the whole time, we were so happy to see each other. Then Mommy and Daddy presented Roczen with a late Christmas gift. It was a teddy bear with a mouse on its shoulder that recited, "It was the Night Before Christmas." The teddy bear's head moved back and forth as he was reciting the poem. Roczen was so happy to get the gift that he immediately hugged the teddy bear tight. He also put his nose close to the bear's nose, and moved back and forth with the teddy bear's head. Mommy took pictures of everything, and said it was the best part of our memorable trip.

The adults sat around and talked for hours. The manager came and introduced himself, as Mac. Mommy confirmed to him that I was a service dog and had a letter to prove it. I guess restaurants have strict rules about dogs inside the restaurant. Danielle told Mac how we met, and he was amazed that it was the High Five between Roczen and myself that joined our families together. Mac looked sad when Danielle told him Roczen had suffered a stroke when he was five days old and lost mobility in his right side. Roczen still can't speak, but his signing skills are excellent. She showed the brace that Roczen is now wearing to help him walk and advised that he is a candidate for a new brace which will help him even more. He then asked about Roczen's prognosis for his recovery. Danielle relayed that last week Roczen was taken back to the clinical study program, and they advised her that there has been a remarkable improvement in his recovery process. After we took photos of all of us, Mac left us to visit some more and advised us that we could stay as long as we liked. I was ecstatic as that allowed more time for Roczen and me to play.

NTER
NDER

Danielle told Mommy that this coming week was a sad time for her as it was the second anniversary of her daughter's passing, which was Roczen's mommy. Danielle is great as a substitute mommy for Roczen, and now instead of calling her his grandmother, he calls her his mommy. The love between the two of them was beautiful to watch. Roczen was great with AJ, or should I say AJ was great with Roczen. AJ takes care of Roczen when his mother works, and according to Danielle a real blessing. AJ let us know that she has family in Buffalo, and Mommy invited everyone to come for a visit, which they promised they would.

We said our goodbyes amid promises to stay in touch. As we were all hugging on the sidewalk, Roczen held his hands up to give us a hug. He really is a good hugger. We looked as they walked away, and were sad to see them go. Mommy did text Danielle the next day after we left the hotel to let her know how much we enjoyed visiting with all of them and looked forward to staying in touch.

I'll write more to you after we stay at that Hampton, and then will definitely get in touch with you when we get home.

By the way, in answer to the question you asked me a while back, why I didn't tell you what Sherman confided to me? I'm waiting to get home, ask you what you think our purpose in life is, and afterward I will share his wisdom with you.

Wuff you. High Five

Hi Zora,

I can't wait. I'm counting down the minutes. I know it's only been a couple of weeks since you've been gone, but it feels like years. Humans say time flies, but for me, it's been standing still. I'm excited on two counts. One, that I get to spend some overdue time with you, and two, that I finally get to find out what it was that Sherman shared with you. Our lives have been meshed together through our families, and I can't recall any year that you and I haven't spent time together. We are both at the same point in our lives, moving slower, sleeping more, and playing less.

Like you, I'm not a quitter. When I have aches and pains, I slow down a bit. I don't complain like some of these fur babies around me. My take is that they are looking for more attention. You and I only bother our parents when we have to go outside, and when it's time to eat. Other than that, I think we are self-sufficient.

Please let me know as soon as you get home. We will have to plan a visit and spend some catch-up, quality time together. Miss you more, even though I know it won't be long now. Love you, Cuz.

Hi Roxy,

The last leg of the trip was uneventful. Mommy mapped out the distance between our home and where we were and decided that Weston, West Virginia, was the halfway point to home.

The Hampton Inn in Weston is really nice, and the people are friendly. Due to the construction on the road, it took us longer than the projected six hours to get to the hotel. After we checked in, my parents got me settled in with my favorite bed throw, gave me my food, took me for a longer walk than usual, and then they left to go out to eat found out later from them that they went to the Outback which was near the hotel. They said their waiter Mike was very friendly and had a good sense of humor. I guess he had to as he was the one who greeted them at the reservation desk, took them to their booth, and waited on them for both their drink order and their food order. He mentioned they were short-handed. No surprise there as that was the same complaint we heard at the various hotels and restaurants we visited along the route.

Before we left that morning, Mommy spoke to the young lady taking care of our rooms, Bekah. Bekah swooped down and grabbed me in her arms giving me a great big hug. She smelled so nice. Mommy told her it was one of the cleanest and nicest hotels so far on this trip. Mommy also told her she was glad that the Hamptons were pet friendly. I took exception to that remark because I choose to believe I'm a member of the family and not just a pet. However. Mommy was right, they were very welcoming. It was so nice to know that other hotels are recognizing that we are an important part of our families.

That said, we are now driving through Pennsylvania, and are not far from Erie. We didn't have the same problem around Pittsburg, as we did on the trip down. Mommy thinks we should be home by seven this evening. I can't wait to sleep in my own bed. If you don't mind, I won't call you tonight. We are planning to come and visit you tomorrow. Mommy already checked with Sissy, and she said that she was looking forward to the visit. Only one more day, and I can share Sherman's wisdom with you.

Wuff you. High Five.

EPILOGUE

The visit between Zora and Roxy was a sight to behold. The two hugged each other, licked each other, and then laid down next to each other. Zora did ask Roxy what she thought her purpose in life was. Roxy answered pretty much like all the fur babies did before. It's to be an important part of the family by letting her family know when someone was coming to the door. She was protecting them. The rest of the answer was the same, to love them, to cuddle them, to play with them, and to be their constant companion. To not let strangers in, and to be polite to their visitors. Not making a nuisance of herself.

Zora and Roxy then laughed, because in their earlier years they both thought it was cute to beg for food, but unfortunately their parents read the book about raising babies, both human and fur.

Then Zora came close to Roxy, hugged her, and whispered into her ear, for you my dear friend, I will share the wisdom

Sherman gave me. We will always be part of our families' lives, and here's the reason why.

One day we were chosen to be their friend,
Their faithful companion until the end.
We will listen, and give them endless love,
Then we will tell them what we learned from above.

Somewhere over the rainbow Bluebirds fly,
Birds fly over the rainbow, and someday so will I.
Someday over the rainbow, we'll meet once more,
I'll be over the rainbow greeting you at the door.